# Foreword

**Councillor Chris Ho**
The Right Worshipful
Lord Mayor of the City & County of Swansea

LIKE many I have fond memories of the Mumbles trains rattling their way around Swansea Bay. I also share the sadness that the railway no longer contributes to Swansea's transport scene or acts as a tourist asset.

The railway provided one of Wales's greatest stories of innovation and daring and it is a delight to contribute the foreword to a book that refreshes the memory and retells the tale with a fascinating pictorial trip on the line in what is a landmark year.

March 25, 2007, marked the 200th anniversary of the world's first passenger carrying railway and *Rocking Rolling Riding* is a commendable salute to what a few years before had only been an industrial line. The switch to a passenger role was an act of genius and proof that Swansea can be a world leader. The coastal railway saw South Wales lead the way into an exciting new age of travel.

Spanning the whole of its history, the book contains many fresh images offering a compelling backdrop to the words of railway and tramway enthusiast David Beynon.

*Rocking Rolling Riding* has been produced, designed and published by social history specialist Bryngold Books, founded by former journalist David Roberts, whose name needs no introduction when it comes to pictures from the past. Together, the pair have given us a book to treasure. As for the title? Well, if you ever had the privilege to travel on the railway then rocking, rolling, riding is exactly the way it was. It is good to look back on how we travelled in the past and with Swansea working hard to enhance its 21st Century passenger transport systems with some ground-breaking new ideas it is interesting to draw a parallel with the Mumbles Railway.

Given that the only surviving relic of the railway is the front of one of its cars at Swansea Museum's Tramway Centre this book is like a ticket to travel back in time.

For many it will be an unforgettable journey. ○

# About the author

DAVID Beynon grew up in 1950s Swansea when many took the Mumbles Railway for granted. It was always there — a part of the townscape, a fact of life.

For David the schoolboy it was a rare treat to get as far as Mumbles on a day out, and to ride a train that linked his home town with the popular resort village of Mumbles. Some pals at the town centre Dynevor Grammar School which he too attended lived on the coastal strip west of Swansea. In his young mind they were lucky to travel by the railway five days a week. Such speed, such style!

The Mumbles Railway helped trigger a lifelong fascination with transport. His interests include many aspects of transport, including the street tramways of Swansea.

# An appreciation

THE compilation of this fresh and fascinating pictorial salute to the world's first passenger railway was possible only with the enthusiastic collaboration of the many who shared the images reproduced on its pages.

The support and encouragement of Ray Lewis, a long-time Swansea exile whose memories of the Mumbles Railway remain strong, are of particular note.

Thanks are also due to: the late Wynne Harris who would have been delighted to see some of his photographs in print; Ken Reeves; John Peake, custodian of Oystermouth Model Railway Club; Tony Cottle and the Mumbles Railway Society; Gerald Gabb, Bernice Cardy and staff at Swansea Museum.

The origin of some pictures is unclear, but whoever stood behind the lens played their part too in keeping the memory of the Mumbles Train alive. We hope this book does too.

# All aboard!

**David Beynon**
Swansea, 2007

IT'S a tale of desire, world firsts, innovation, change and success. Throw in a lively mix of local pride and occasional controversy and you have the Mumbles Railway.

The story continues to run — unlike the trains — so there are three other vital elements to factor in: a sad loss, colourful memories and animated debate.

This wonderful coastal line began life more than two centuries ago as the Oystermouth Tramroad or Railway.

Later it became The Swansea and Mumbles Railway and then The Mumbles Pier and Railway Company.

Horse-drawn vehicles, steam engines and electric power all played their part. The line flourished under the ownership of the Swansea Improvements and Tramways Company and later, South Wales Transport.

The last trains ran in January 1960, but many decades later the people of Swansea retain a passion for their rail pioneers and for the services they offered.

Such fondness is reflected in the title of this book, for rocking, rolling, riding is just what passengers did when they travelled on the Mumbles Railway.

For the most part the pictures in this book tell their own story. They follow the route taken by many who travelled the line in later years — from Rutland Street terminus to the entertainment paradise that was Mumbles Pier.

The numerous stations that existed along the line are visited and those who look closely will find all 13 electric cars are in evidence.

*Rocking Rolling Riding* is a pictorial salute to what has to be one of the world's great transport stories.

It will trigger memories and stimulate new interest in the first passenger railway.

All aboard!

# Horse power
# 1804-1877

STRANGE as it may seem, there was no coastal road between Swansea and Mumbles as the 19th century dawned. This meant difficulties for those transporting quarried limestone from the Mumbles area and coal from the Clyne Valley to the embryonic port of Swansea.

To tackle the problem, the Oystermouth Railway or Tramroad Company was formed in 1804. Construction work on a Swansea to Mumbles line began in September 1805, and the first wagons rolled the following April.

Pulled by horses, they carried minerals, limestone and coal. In 1807, following a proposal by Benjamin French, this beach-side route became the first railway in the world to carry advertised passenger trains. Specially adapted wagons were provided but the horses remained.

Visitors flocked to see and experience this inspirational novelty. Horses were the sole providers of haulage until a sequence of events started with the passing, in 1874, of the Swansea Tramways & Improvements Act.

Powers obtained under this, allowed the Swansea Improvements & Tramways Company, to construct Swansea's street tramway system and buy, lease or, acquire the Mumbles Railway.

By 1877, much of the line had been completely upgraded and relaid in readiness for the expected increase in traffic derived from connecting the railway with the town tramways network. A year later horses were forced to share with a competing power source, one that had taken over completely by the mid-1890s.

That power was steam.

A mix of horse-drawn vehicles was in use on the Mumbles Railway. Here an early single deck, two horse carriage is posed for the camera near Ashleigh Road.

A double deck carriage prepares to leave the original western terminus of the line at The Elms, Oystermouth. The little girl at the end of the platform appears more interested in the photographer.

This is how passengers travelled the line in the 1860s. First class ticket holders went inside, second class outside and on the less comfortable, open to the elements, upper deck knifeboard seating.

# MAY, 1869.

# SWANSEA AND MUMBLES.

## Oystermouth Railway Time Table.

### DOWN TRAINS

| FARES Single 1st | Single 2nd | Return 1st | Return 2nd | DOWN TRAINS | WEEK DAYS mrn | mrn | mrn | aft | aft | aft | aft | aft | aft | aft | SATURDAYS (EXTRA) mrn | SUNDAYS mrn | mrn | aft | aft | aft | aft |
|---|---|---|---|---|---|---|---|---|---|---|---|---|---|---|---|---|---|---|---|---|---|
| 4d | 3d | 6d | 4d | SWANSEA, Rutland-street | 6 0 | 8 0 | 10 0 | 12 30 | 2 0 | 3 0 | 4 0 | 5 20 | 7 0 | 8 30 | 9 0 | 6 0 | 10 0 | 2 0 | 3 0 | 6 0 | 8 30 |
| | | | | St. Helen's Road | 6 8 | 8 8 | 10 8 | 12 38 | 2 8 | 3 8 | 4 8 | 5 28 | 7 8 | 8 38 | 9 8 | 6 8 | 10 8 | 2 8 | 3 8 | 6 8 | 8 38 |
| | | | | Water Works Road | 6 12 | 8 12 | 10 12 | 12 42 | 2 12 | 3 12 | 4 12 | 5 32 | 7 12 | 8 42 | 9 12 | 6 12 | 10 12 | 2 12 | 3 12 | 6 12 | 8 42 |
| | | | | Sketty Road | 6 16 | 8 16 | 10 16 | 12 46 | 2 16 | 3 16 | 4 16 | 5 36 | 7 16 | 8 46 | 9 16 | 6 16 | 10 16 | 2 16 | 3 16 | 6 16 | 8 46 |
| | | | | Black Pill Road / Bishopston Road | 6 25 | 8 25 | 10 25 | 12 55 | 2 25 | 3 25 | 4 25 | 5 45 | 7 25 | 8 55 | 9 25 | 6 25 | 10 25 | 2 25 | 3 25 | 6 25 | 8 55 |
| 5d | 4d | 8d | 6d | Lilliput Road | 6 30 | 8 30 | 10 30 | 1 0 | 2 30 | 3 30 | 4 30 | 5 50 | 7 30 | 9 0 | 9 30 | 6 30 | 10 30 | 2 30 | 3 30 | 6 30 | 9 0 |
| | | | | West Cross Road / Norton Road | 6 33 | 8 33 | 10 33 | 1 3 | 2 33 | 3 33 | 4 33 | 5 53 | 7 33 | 9 3 | 9 33 | 6 33 | 10 33 | 2 33 | 3 33 | 6 33 | 9 3 |
| 7d | 5d | 10d | 6d | MUMBLES | 6 43 | 8 43 | 10 43 | 1 13 | 2 43 | 3 43 | 4 43 | 6 3 | 7 43 | 9 13 | 9 43 | 6 43 | 10 43 | 2 43 | 3 43 | 6 43 | 9 13 |

### UP TRAINS

| FARES Single 1st | Single 2nd | Return 1st | Return 2nd | UP TRAINS | WEEK DAYS mrn | mrn | mrn | aft | aft | aft | aft | aft | aft | SATURDAYS (EXTRA) mrn | SUNDAYS mrn | aft | aft | aft | aft |
|---|---|---|---|---|---|---|---|---|---|---|---|---|---|---|---|---|---|---|---|
| 4d | 3d | 6d | 4d | MUMBLES | 9 0 | 10 0 | 11 0 | 2 0 | 3 0 | 4 0 | 5 0 | 7 0 | 8 30 | 8 0 | 10 0 | 1 0 | 5 0 | 7 0 | 8 30 |
| | | | | Norton Road / West Cross Road | 9 10 | 10 10 | 11 10 | 2 10 | 3 10 | 4 10 | 5 10 | 7 10 | 8 40 | 8 10 | 10 10 | 1 10 | 5 10 | 7 10 | 8 40 |
| | | | | Lilliput Road | 9 13 | 10 13 | 11 13 | 2 13 | 3 13 | 4 13 | 5 13 | 7 13 | 8 43 | 8 13 | 10 13 | 1 13 | 5 13 | 7 13 | 8 43 |
| | | | | Bishopston Road / Black Pill Road | 9 18 | 10 18 | 11 18 | 2 18 | 3 18 | 4 18 | 5 18 | 7 18 | 8 48 | 8 18 | 10 18 | 1 18 | 5 18 | 7 18 | 8 48 |
| 5d | 4d | 8d | 6d | Sketty Road | 9 23 | 10 23 | 11 23 | 2 23 | 3 23 | 4 23 | 5 23 | 7 23 | 8 53 | 8 23 | 10 23 | 1 23 | 5 23 | 7 23 | 8 53 |
| | | | | Water Works Road | 9 27 | 10 27 | 11 27 | 2 27 | 3 27 | 4 27 | 5 27 | 7 27 | 8 57 | 8 27 | 10 27 | 1 27 | 5 27 | 7 27 | 8 57 |
| 7d | 5d | 10d | 6d | St. Helen's Road | 9 35 | 10 35 | 11 35 | 2 35 | 3 35 | 4 35 | 5 35 | 7 35 | 9 5 | 8 35 | 10 35 | 1 35 | 5 35 | 7 35 | 9 5 |
| | | | | SWANSEA, Rutland-street | 9 43 | 10 43 | 11 43 | 2 43 | 3 43 | 4 43 | 5 43 | 7 43 | 9 13 | 8 43 | 10 43 | 1 43 | 5 43 | 7 43 | 9 13 |

For Conveyance of Goods, Hire of **SPECIAL CARRIAGES**, and **SALE OF TICKETS**, at a **DISCOUNT**, apply to Mr. R. WILLIAMS, at the Station, Rutland Street, Swansea.

NOTICE.—To TOURISTS and VISITORS.—THE MUMBLES is replete with every accommodation for Visitors, picturesquely situated in the

One of the older single horse, double deck carriages which plied the line until the advent of steam. Unusually, the upper deck was not fitted with decency boards to hide the ankles and the blushes of its women passengers.

With two women sitting alongside the driver, a well loaded double-deck coach leaves Oystermouth for Swansea in the 1860s. Two policemen appear to have hitched a ride on the running board of the two horse vehicle.

The two youngsters seated on the driver's bench would no doubt have been delighted with their prestigious position for the trip into Swansea from the Mumbles terminus.

# Steam locomotion
# 1878-1929

**G**REAT tension gripped Swansea in the 1870s as steam technology challenged a decades-old Mumbles Railway monopoly enjoyed by horse power. The Swansea Improvements and Tramways Company had been tasked with installing street tramways across the town and linking the new services with the Mumbles Railway.

Negotiations with the railway's owners saw much of the line upgraded and a new depot built on the site of today's Crown Court. The year 1878 brought a successful trial of a steam locomotive. It led to the buying of a further two, but a legal battle between the two companies resulted in the tramway company having to revert to horse power.

The railway enterprise pushed ahead with steam and prospered. For some time this meant steam engines and horse power on the same line. Stormy relations existed between the companies until 1896 when tramways bosses abandoned their right to run horse-drawn trains on the line. Steam had seen off its rival. The Mumbles Railway usually had four or five steam locomotives on its books. They worked chimney first when going to Mumbles, cab first when returning to Swansea, probably to provide as much protection as possible against the worst of the prevailing weather.

A look-out person would sit on the footplate, charged with warning the driver of obstructions or oncoming trains.

The locomotives were quite small but easily coped with the heavy loads. On Bank Holidays and summer weekends they would pull trains of a dozen or more double-deck coaches containing around 1,300 passengers. Even though the line was nearly level for its full length, this was still some feat. Steam, however, was ultimately to be toppled by an exciting new power source.

It was the start of the Mumbles Railway's electric age.

Some of the first passengers on the steam hauled Mumbles Railway. Pictured at Rutland Street terminus in 1877 the train is being hauled by Progress, an enclosed steam locomotive, that compared to many was relatively noise and steam free. Its top speed was around 8mph.

A driver and fireman take a break from their duties while passengers board a Mumbles-bound train hauled by locomotive No. 3 at Rutland Street terminus during the early 1920s.

**Saddle tank locomotive Swansea eases its carriages into Rutland Street station, the Swansea terminus for passenger trains, in readiness for its journey to Mumbles. The overhead masts and wires are ready for the start of electric traction in 1929.**

**With steam to spare locomotive No. 5
stands ready for duty outside the
Rutland Street depot.**

**Passengers pile into what were affectionately referred to as cattle trucks in readiness for an
excursion to Mumbles. The wagons seen here outside Argyle Street carriage shed were often used
for special trips or during busy periods.**

Not a bare head to be seen! Hats were definitely the order of the day as hundreds of Edwardian passengers clamber aboard the train at Rutland Street heading for an afternoon enjoying the attractions offered by Mumbles and its pier.

Those same passengers would have enjoyed a grandstand view of the entertainment offered on Swansea Sands as they passed the Slip. The Bay View Hotel towers behind them.

**In summertime space was always at a premium for those seeking a train ride to Mumbles.**

On one busy bank holiday a steam-hauled Mumbles train is reputed to have rattled into the record books with 1,800 passengers on board. This packed train at the Slip in 1920 shows how they would probably have travelled.

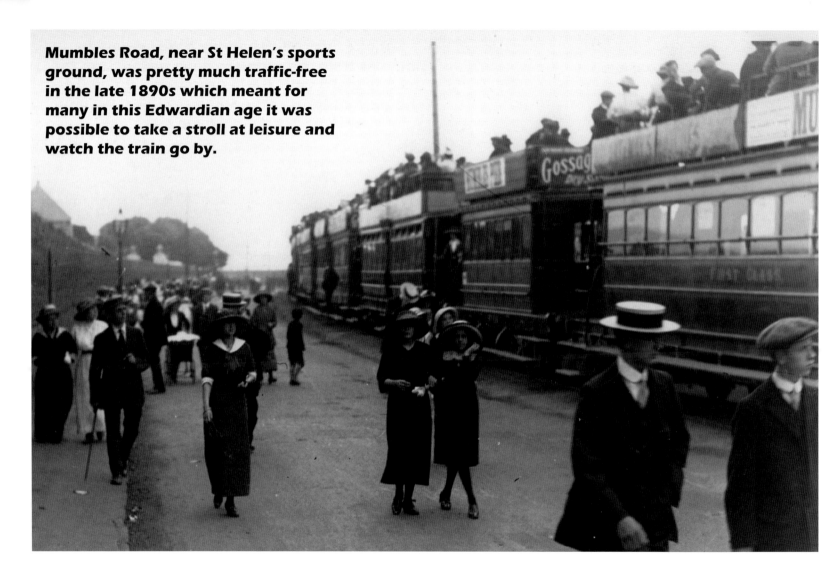

Mumbles Road, near St Helen's sports ground, was pretty much traffic-free in the late 1890s which meant for many in this Edwardian age it was possible to take a stroll at leisure and watch the train go by.

This train is packed to capacity as it passes St Helen's sports ground heading for Mumbles, 1914. With a look-out man on the front of the locomotive, it is about to arrive at St Gabriel's station.

Two young boys perform tricks in anticipation of being thrown coins by the top deck passengers on this slow moving train near St Gabriel's station. It seems cycling was the next most popular form of transport on this fine day.

Locomotive No. 4 passes St Gabriel's loop as it heads for Mumbles during the summer of 1899. Once again it appears packed to capacity — except that is for the carriage immediately behind the tank engine which was used for conveying workmen.

**Summertime crowds flock towards a recently arrived train of mixed carriages at Brynmill, hoping to have a ride to Mumbles and a chance to experience its delights.**

A flag man guards the access to the beach at Brynmill while passengers board the train, 1912. The locomotive look-out man surveys the scene patiently.

Looking down Brynmill Lane at a passing train. The middle carriage is a former Swansea street tram.

A close-up of one of the wagons, affectionately known as cattle trucks, used for excursions and at busy times. This one is at the end of a Mumbles-bound train. The seating was at best, basic.

Shake, rattle and roll at its best! The steam from the locomotive chimney and the differing angles of the carriages gives the impression that the train was travelling much faster than the eight miles an hour it was limited to.

Children watch as a train passes by at Blackpill. Not surprisingly perhaps, this type of carriage was referred to as a toast rack.

**Before the laying of a new route along the shoreline by the Mumbles Railway and Pier Company, the track followed the road between Blackpill and Oystermouth. The pony and trap here has been brought to a halt by its driver while a train passes. Alongside him another horse-drawn vehicle can be seen entering the driveway of one of the large houses that stood along this stretch of road.**

In 1888, the Mumbles Railway & Pier Company was formed to extend the line from Oystermouth to Mumbles Head and build the pier. The extended line by-passed the original terminus at Oystermouth and in 1893 was opened as far as Southend. With construction work still underway, this train is standing at the new Oystermouth station.

**Day trippers returning home from Mumbles. An oyster dredger rests in the lay-up built by the Mumbles Railway and Pier Company to replace moorings lost when the line was extended.**

A sunny day and the tide is in full flow as a saddle tank locomotive arrives at Mumbles Pier with a packed train and prepares to discharge its cargo of excited passengers.

Locomotive No. 5 and its driver enjoy a break from their labours while they wait to leave Mumbles Pier station on their return trip to Swansea.

A train from Swansea arrives at the pier. The fashions worn by the two women suggest a warm day. The people with their backs to the camera are waiting to board the train for its return journey to Swansea.

# Electric traction
# 1929-1960

THE heyday of the Mumbles Railway really began with the opening of the pier in 1898. A year later its operation passed to the Swansea Improvements and Tramways Company.

Meanwhile, Swansea celebrated a notable first in 1900 when it became the first Welsh town to have electric tram cars on its streets. It was a sign of things to come for the steam-powered Mumbles Railway. Indeed, only cost factors stopped it switching to electric power before the First World War.

The post-war years produced new calls for electricity. Mumbles and its pier had become increasingly popular and were largely responsible for growth of the railway. Large numbers of summertime day trippers in long, slow steam trains caused operational problems. In 1927, the South Wales Transport bus company took over the railway.

Electric power soon followed. Eleven tramway-type cars were ordered. They were the largest in Britain, each providing seating 106 passengers, and could run coupled together allowing their legitimate description as trains. Two more cars, numbers 12 and 13, arrived as passenger numbers grew.

The livery of the early cars matched that of the town's tramcars — cream with a plum coloured lower body and banding.

In the mid-1930s red cars with cream banding and white roofs became more familiar. In style, these matched the buses of South Wales Transport.

After busy times throughout the Second World War the line and its cars both needed significant upgrading. A decision had to be made on whether to invest or close, leaving the route open to more modern diesel-powered buses.

Sadly, despite a concerted campaign by its supporters the railway lost.

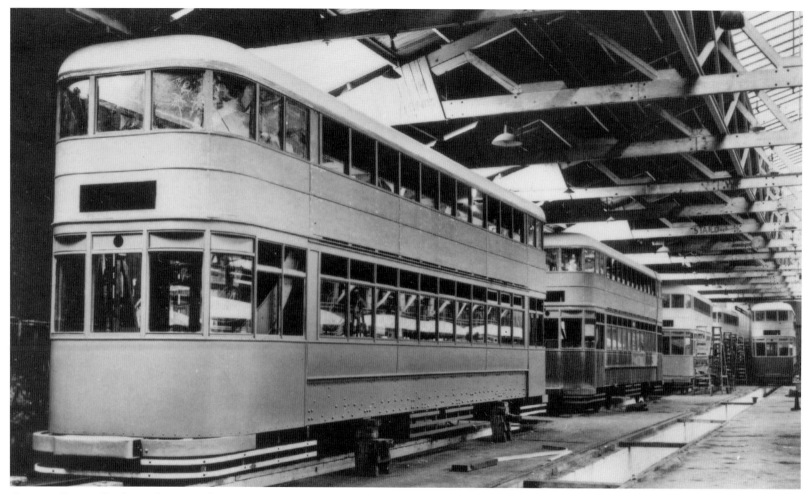

A number of electric cars for the Mumbles Railway in various stages of construction at the Brush company's works at Loughborough, Leicestershire.

The reason these vehicles were called trains and not trams was that they could operate coupled together. Here, a two car train in its original livery colours waits to leave the Rutland Street terminus.

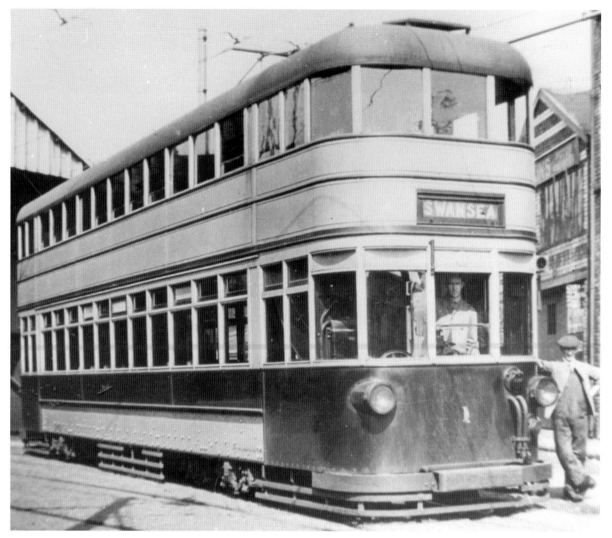

**Car No. 1 stands outside Rutland Street car shed. It was delivered painted in the same maroon and cream colours as the town's tram cars.**

**An atmospheric early morning view along Oystermouth Road that modern motorists can only dream of. A solitary car makes its way into town along the cobbled roadway as car No. 13 with one of its crewmen waits patiently for its first passengers of the day for Mumbles.**

## The South Wales Transport Company Ltd.

### The Service of Electric Trains on the

# MUMBLES RAILWAY

#### commenced on the 2nd of MARCH, 1929

Until Further Notice the Following Experimental Service will be Operated:

| FROM RUTLAND ST., SWANSEA. Week Days. | FROM MUMBLES PIER. Week Days. |
|---|---|
| A.M.—4.35, 5.40, 6.29, 7.15, 7.42, 7.51, 8.0, 8.9, 8.27, 8.36, 8.45, 9.3, 9.30, 9.57, 10.24, 10.51, 11.18, 11.45. | A.M.—5.0, 6.5, 6.52, 7.40, 8.7, 8.16, 8.25, 8.31, 8.52, 9.1, 9.10, 9.28, 9.55, 10.22, 10.49, 11.16, 11.43. |
| P.M.—12.12, 12.39, 12.57, 1.6, 1.15, 1.33, 1.51, 2.0, 2.27, 2.54, 3.21, 3.48, 4.15, 4.24, 4.42, 4.51, 5.9, 5.18, 5.36, 5.45, 6.3, 6.12, 6.30, 6.57, 7.24, 7.51, 8.18, 8.45, 9.12, 9.39, 10.6, 10.33, 11. | P.M.—12.10, 12.37, 1.4, 1.22, 1.31, 1.58, 2.7, 2.16, 2.25, 2.52, 3.19, 3. 4.13, 4.40, 4.49, 5.7, 5.16, 5.5 5.43, 6.1, 6.10, 6.28, 6.37, 6.55, 22, 7.49, 8.16, 8.43, 9.10, 9.37, 1.4, 10.31, 10.58, 11.25. |

### FARES—ALL ONE CLASS.

| | SINGLE. | | | | | | | | | RETURN. | | | | | |
|---|---|---|---|---|---|---|---|---|---|---|---|---|---|---|---|
| | Rutland St. | St. Helen's | Brynmill | Ashleigh Rd. | Blackpill | West Cross | Norton Rd. | Oystermouth | Southend | Mumbles Pier | Ashleigh Rd. | Blackpill | West Cross | Norton Rd. | Oystermouth | Southend | Mumbles Pier |
| Rutland Street | ... | 2 | 3 | 4 | 4 | 5 | 6 | 6 | 7 | 7 | 7 | 7 | 9 | 10 | 10 | 1/- | 1/- |
| St. Helen's | ... | ... | 2 | 3 | 3 | 5 | 6 | 6 | 7 | 7 | 5 | 5 | 9 | 10 | 10 | 1/- | 1/- |
| Brynmill | ... | ... | ... | 2 | 2 | 4 | 5 | 5 | 6 | 6 | ... | ... | 7 | 9 | 9 | 10 | 10 |

**An impressive line-up of cars ready for service at Rutland Street depot.**

**Cars 3, 7, 1 and 6 at rest in the shelter of Rutland Street depot. Catwalks suspended from the roof enabled easy cleaning of the upper deck windows.**

A conductor walks across the road to the office at Rutland Street station to pay in his takings while the driver returns car No. 4 to the depot.

A lone cyclist makes his way along Oystermouth Road while in the background two Mumbles trains pass each other at Argyle Street loop.

**Young conductor Tommy Jackson stands alongside car No. 1 at Rutland Street station during the summer of 1959.**

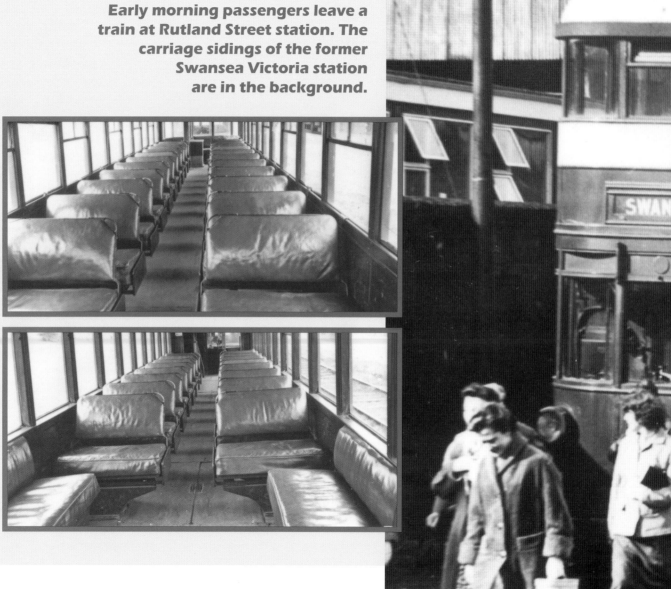

Early morning passengers leave a train at Rutland Street station. The carriage sidings of the former Swansea Victoria station are in the background.

These are the blue leather seats that passengers on either deck would have sat on. The backs could be folded over to allow people to face the direction of travel or to chat with one another.

In the mid-1930s, the electric cars lost their original Swansea street tram livery and were repainted in the same style as the South Wales Transport Company's bus fleet. Here in a typical early 1950s scene passengers are boarding a two-car train at Rutland Street terminus. Car No. 1 would soon be leading the way as it rumbled along to Mumbles Pier.

Argyle Street loop, opposite the gasworks which later became the site of a Tesco supermarket. Merriman & Stephens' coal depot can be seen on the right of this view eastwards along Oystermouth Road.

The station at the Slip was named in the railway's timetables as St Helen's. It boasted a shop and waiting shelter. On the left is the neighbouring LMS railway line's signal box which controlled the level crossing allowing access to Swansea beach.

**A drop of oil worked wonders for keeping the world's oldest passenger-carrying railway on track — and on time.**

**A two car train passes Trafalgar Arch as it heads towards Rutland Street on its return from Mumbles, mid-1950s.**

A single car train passes under the Slip bridge as it approaches St Helen's station. Only the piers of the bridge remain to show that there were once the lines of two railway companies running almost side by side here.

Car No. 2 heads away from the Slip with a train for Mumbles. On the far side of the LMS Swansea to Shrewsbury railway line, can be seen the café on stilts which provided meals and jugs of tea for beachgoers for many decades.

**Two trains pass one another at St Gabriel's loop on a typical wet winter's day, 1958.**

Street lights mimic the graceful curve of Swansea Bay with their illuminations on a late summer's evening as a train travels between Swansea Bay railway station and the Slip.

A two car train to Mumbles enters St Gabriel's loop, opposite St Helen's rugby and cricket ground, where it would halt for a Swansea-bound train, carrying the photographer, to pass. Beyond the loop there was only a single track as far as Sketty Lane.

Two trains pass at St Gabriel's loop on a busy, late 1950s summer's afternoon.

The Mumbles Railway was brought to a standstill on Whitsun Monday, April 19, 1954, following this accident near the bottom of Brynmill Lane. With an ambulance in attendance, crowds thronged the scene of the incident, which appeared to involve a two car train and a vehicle crossing the line.

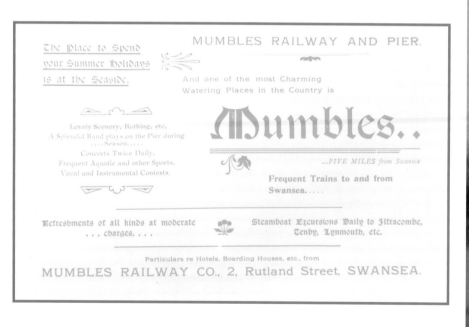

MUMBLES RAILWAY AND PIER.

The Place to Spend your Summer Holidays is at the Seaside.

And one of the most Charming Watering Places in the Country is

# Mumbles..

Lovely Scenery, Bathing, etc.
A Splendid Band plays on the Pier during ....Season.....
Concerts Twice Daily.
Frequent Aquatic and other Sports.
Vocal and Instrumental Contests.

...FIVE MILES *from Swansea*

Frequent Trains to and from Swansea.....

Refreshments of all kinds at moderate ... charges. ....

Steamboat Excursions Daily to Ilfracombe, Tenby, Lynmouth, etc.

Particulars re Hotels, Boarding Houses, etc., from

MUMBLES RAILWAY CO., 2, Rutland Street, SWANSEA.

**A quiet Mumbles Road, showing the railway sandwiched between the promenade and the roadway alongside the Recreation Ground, mid-1950s.**

A roll call of stations along the route after 1929. By this time St Gabriel's station was no longer in use.

Rutland Street

Argyle Street

St. Helens

Brynmill

Ashleigh Road

Blackpill

West Cross

Norton Road

Oystermouth

Southend

Pier

**Car No. 12, heading for Mumbles, has just passed another returning to Swansea on the double track section of line between Sketty Lane and Blackpill.**

**Fares please! Conductor Bill Allsopp with his ticket machine and money bag during the mid-1950s.**

. . . And here's the kind of weekly ticket with which regular passengers were issued when they rode on the electric train.

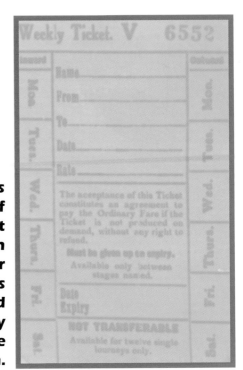

Weekly Ticket. V 6552

Issued | | Unissued
Mon. | Name........ | Mon.
 | From........ |
Tues. | To........ | Tues.
 | Date........ |
Wed. | Rate........ | Wed.
 | The acceptance of this Ticket constitutes an agreement to pay the Ordinary Fare if the Ticket is not produced on demand, without any right to refund. |
Thurs. | | Thurs.
 | Must be given up on expiry. |
 | Available only between stages named. |
Fri. | Date Expiry | Fri.
 | NOT TRANSFERABLE |
Sat. | Available for twelve single journeys only. | Sat.

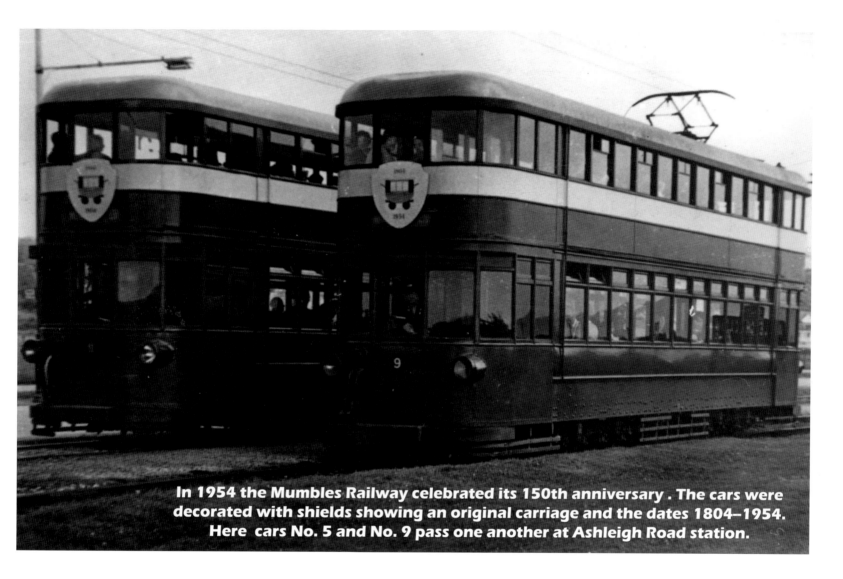

In 1954 the Mumbles Railway celebrated its 150th anniversary . The cars were decorated with shields showing an original carriage and the dates 1804–1954. Here cars No. 5 and No. 9 pass one another at Ashleigh Road station.

**An AEC Regent V double deck bus with Mumbles Pier on its destination board passes Car No. 2 bound for Southend, where the line then terminated. This 1959 scene at Ashleigh Road illustrates the brief period when both train and bus services were in operation.**

**Showing the wrong destination — Swansea — Car No. 10 passes King George V playing fields on its way to Mumbles.**

A two car train approaching Blackpill station having just emerged from under the bridge carrying the former LMS railway line from Swansea Victoria station to Shrewsbury.

On July 8, 1959, two double car trains collided on the single track near Blackpill station. A shuttle service was operated either side of the damaged trains. Under the watchful eyes of the local police, passengers walk past the damaged cars to board the train waiting on the other side of the railway bridge to take them to Swansea.

**The impressive electricity sub-station at Blackpill. Now a popular cafe, it is one of the few reminders of the Mumbles Railway that remain. It was built shortly before electrification in 1929.**

**A summertime scene at Blackpill station with the crowded lido alongside.**

**A Swansea-bound train halts at West Cross station while the passing loop allows one headed for Mumbles and the pier to continue on its way.**

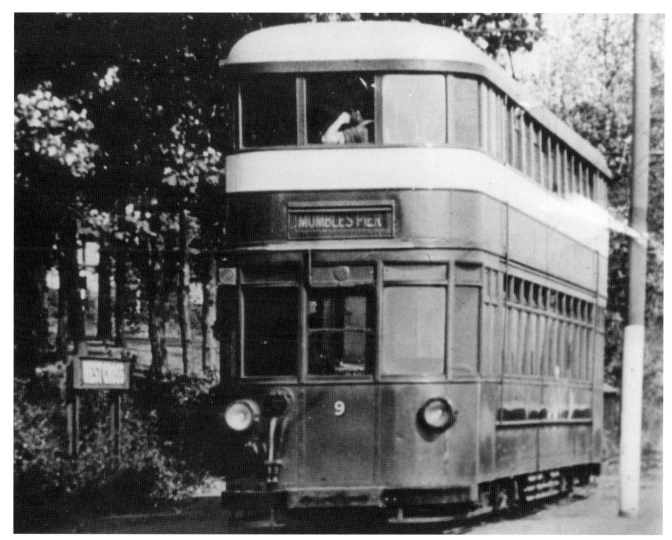

**Car No. 9 draws to a halt at West Cross station.**

**With the houses alongside Mumbles Road just visible in the background Car No. 1 runs between West Cross and Norton Road stations on a mid-1950s summer's afternoon.**

**Converted horse tram bodies, redundant after the town's tramways were electrified in 1900, were originally used as waiting shelters at Mumbles Railway stations. Later, they were replaced by the type of building seen here at Norton Road station.**

**The crew of car No. 10 stand proudly alongside their charge at Mumbles.**

**A peep at the controls inside the motorman's cab.**

The word Southend on the destination board of car No. 10 as it arrived at Oystermouth station in late 1959 is an ominous clue to the fact that by then the line to the pier had already been closed.

The arrival of car No. 3 with passengers headed for Mumbles Pier is greeted with a wave from a group of youngsters at Oystermouth.

Nearly there! Car No. 4 and its partner, their doors closed, all set to depart from Oystermouth station for the last part of their journey to the pier.

Southend was the only station to have a footbridge crossing the line. It can be seen in the background as a single car train for Swansea arrives there during the late 1950s.

The last car delivered to the Mumbles Railway — No. 13 — passes laid-up boats at Southend on its way to Swansea.

The holiday feeling so evident in this atmospheric, mid-1950s view of car No. 10 leaving Southend station for Mumbles Pier is exactly what lured many passengers to ride on the railway during countless Swansea Bay summers.

**Boats are drawn-up on one side of the line and cars parked on the other as passengers alight from a train at Southend station.**

Mumbles Pier was built to resemble the promenade deck of a liner and provided a superb vantage point to watch the arrival and departure of trains as this photograph proves.

The cafe on the right was a popular rendezvous after a bracing walk along the pier or promenade. Perhaps even the crew of car No. 5, seen waiting to begin its return to Swansea had called in for a refreshing cuppa.

It's early in the season at Mumbles Pier and just a few passengers walk away from a recently arrived train. On busy summer days the scene would be far different.

**The cutting and cliffs at Mumbles dwarf a two car train approaching the Pier terminus.**

Leaning into the curve, a train heading for Mumbles Pier passes Knab Rock with the majestic sweep of Swansea Bay behind it.

**The sign on the board says it all.  A general view of Mumbles Pier station, late 1950s.**

Making a welcoming sight on a wet night at Mumbles Pier, a single car waits for late night revellers from the nearby attractions.

**The RNLI boathouse at Mumbles is visible behind car No. 6 as it waits to head a two car train back to Swansea. The Ben Evans department store, advertised on the side of the car was, until it was destroyed in the Three Nights' Blitz of 1941, one of Swansea's shopping hotspots.**

End of the line
1960

THE 1950s saw road transport start to revolutionise the way we lived. But there was a cost. One victim was the Mumbles Railway which, by this time, was being run by bus operator South Wales Transport.

The line was closed in two phases. The first saw the abandonment of the section from Mumbles Pier to Southend.

This allowed the railway owners to convert the short stretch of track bed from the pier to Knab Rock into a road so that the buses working the route could gain access to the pier. Final closure occurred on January 5, 1960. Track and overhead electric equipment were removed and the cars dismantled.

One survived for a short time, having been bought by the Middleton Railway Trust in Leeds. It was later destroyed by fire.

The rail line that had given the world its first passenger railway was no more. It had served the people of Swansea, and millions of visitors, for more than 150 years.

The Sixties might have been swinging for some, but for the rock 'n' rollers who loved travelling on the Mumbles Railway it was a time of mourning.

They organised a wake, dressing in mourning garments. A cortege of cars followed the last train from Swansea to Mumbles and back. People gathered along the route and crowds mobbed the last train to return to the Rutland Street depot.

The only significant remnant of a Mumbles train is housed in Swansea Museum's marina-side Tramway Centre. It's the cab end of electric car No. 7.

What memories it holds!

A procession of cars follows the last service train, decorated with coloured lights and shields, as it passes Ashleigh Road on its return to Swansea, January 5, 1960.

**After the last service train departed from Southend, a group of regular local passengers hired their own train for a wake. Some of the 'mourners' are seen congregating at Southend station.**

**Arrival of the official last train at Southend gave the Deputy Mayor and Mayoress of Swansea a chance to greet the driver — motorman Frank Dunkin who had started work on the railway as a boy.**

As the Mumbles train made its final journey on January 5, 1960, residents of Oystermouth Road turned out in force to wish it a final farewell. For many, leaving their homes had meant crossing the line. Car No. 6 heads this two car train proudly displaying a shield proclaiming the lifespan of the Mumbles Railway — from 1804 to 1960.

Crowds throng the last train as it rumbles back into the Rutland Street depot for the very last time. Swansea had lost an old friend.

A policeman holds back the crowd as the last train arrives at Oystermouth. Many pennies were placed on the line that day to be flattened by the wheels of the train and kept safely as mementos.

BERNARD HASTIE
& CO.LTD.
Insulating Contractors & Sheet-metal Workers

**Car No. 1 and an unidentified partner being dismantled on Argyle Street loop alongside the roadway.**

Cars were dismantled for scrap wherever there was sufficient room. Here work had started on Car No. 3 on the depot tracks at Rutland Street. It wasn't long before the upper deck had vanished completely. (inset)

Rutland Street terminus, late spring 1960. The Mumbles Railway track had already been ripped up. The tram shed in the background looks forlorn. The Mumbles railway office and Hodder's cafe are both now long gone and the roadway much wider at this point.